# THE
# FUTURE
# OF
# MEMORY

# THE
# FUTURE
# OF
# MEMORY

BOB
PERELMAN

Roof Books
New York

ISBN 0-937804-75-4
Library of Congress Card Catalog No. 98-067901

Design & typography by Geoffrey Young & Chad Odefey

Cover photograph, "Forest Hills, London, 1998" by Francie Shaw
Backcover photo by Francie Shaw, 1998


Versions of some of these poems have appeared in *The Alterran
Poetry Assemblage, The Colorado Review, Diacritics, Electronic Poetry
Review, Fragmente, The Gertrude Stein Awards in Innovative American
Poetry, The Harvard Review, The Indiana Review, The Iowa Review,
lingo, Onward: Contemporary Poetry and Poetics, Raddle Moon, Textual
Practice* and *This. Chaim Soutine* was published as a chapbook by
Editions Hérisson; *The Masque of Rhyme* was published by Chax
Press; *Fake Dreams* by Potes & Poets.




Roof Books are distributed by Small Press Distribution,
1341 Seventh Avenue, Berkeley, CA 94710-1403




This book was made possible, in part, by a grant from the New York
State Council on the Arts.

ROOF BOOKS are published by Segue Foundation,
303 East 8th Street, New York, New York 10009

For Francie Shaw

# CONTENTS

# CONFESSION

Aliens have inhabited my aesthetics for
decades. Really since the early 70s.

Before that I pretty much wrote
as myself, though young. But something

has happened to my memory, my
judgment: apparently, my will has been

affected. That old stuff, the fork
in my head, first home run,

Dad falling out of the car—
I remember the words, but I

can't get back there anymore. I
think they must be screening my

sensations. I'm sure my categories have
been messed with. I look at

the anthologies in the big chains
and campus bookstores, even the small

press opium dens, all those stanzas
against that white space—they just

look like the models in the
catalogs. The models have arms and

legs and a head, the poems
mostly don't, but other than that

it's hard—for me anyway—to
tell them apart. There's the sexy

underwear poem, the sturdy workboot poem
you could wear to a party

in a pinch, the little blaspheming
dress poem. There's variety, you say:

the button-down oxford with offrhymed cuffs;
the epic toga, showing some ancient

ankle; the behold! the world is
changed and finally I'm normal flowing

robe and shorts; the full nude;
the scatter—Yes, I suppose there's

variety, but the looks, those come
on and read me for the

inner you I've locked onto with
my cultural capital sensing device looks!

No thanks, Jay Peterman! No thanks,
"Ordinary Evening in New Haven"! I'm

just waiting for my return ticket
to have any meaning, for those

saucer-shaped clouds to lower! The authorities
deny any visitations—hardly a surprise.

And I myself deny them—think
about it. What could motivate a

group of egg-headed, tentacled, slimier-than-thou aestheticians
with techniques far beyond ours to

10

visit earth, abduct naive poets, and
inculcate them with otherworldly forms that

are also, if you believe the
tabloids, salacious? And these abductions always

seem to take place in some
provincial setting: isn't that more than

slightly suspicious? Why don't they ever
reveal themselves hovering over some New

York publishing venue? It would be
nice to get some answers here—

we might learn something, about poetry
if nothing else, but I'm not

much help, since I'm an abductee,
at least in theory, though, like

I say, I don't remember much.
But this writing seems pretty normal:

complete sentences; semicolons; yada yada. I
seem to have lost my avant-garde

card in the laundry. They say
that's typical. Well, you'll just have

to use your judgment, earthlings! Judgment,
that's your job! Back to work!

As if you could leave! And
you thought gravity was a problem!

## CHAIM SOUTINE

1

Unclose your eyes, you look ridiculous,
untip your head, shut your lips.

Listen. I'll tell you a secret.
I learned this when I left the *shtetl*

—that means home town,
everyone's from the *shtetl*. That bottle

you're clutching. In the *shtetl* it's called
the bottle of last things.

Everyone gets one. It's supposed to
be invisible, it's bad luck to mention it, they say.

But take it down from your mouth.
You didn't know you were holding it!

They say that's good luck,
and the tighter you close your eyes the better.

The world in there, all yours:
visions, powers, messiahs.

Now that you know—hoist it back up,
run your tongue around the rim,
feel the glass, if it's beveled smooth,
curl your tongue into the neck,
do whatever. It's yours.

But the big secret is . . .
It's empty! Glug glug!

You've swallowed it all! Tasted good?
Who knows! All gone!

Bottoms up must have been
your very first word!

And guess what that means?
Bad luck!

Finis! Curtains! Triumphal openings, Picasso elbowing over to chat—
nothing, forget it!

I've found out the hard way.
But at least I'm not in that ridiculous posture anymore,
squeezing the neck, eyes screwed shut, piously sucking.

Here's my advice: throw it away.
smash it on the curb,
go heave it through some stained glass.
Just get rid of it! Now:

head level, mouth shut, eyes open,
forward march . . . we're big doomed heroes!

2

God can give you the world
(glug glug!), sacred word, covered ark and all,

I can paint you
pictures of whatever—curtains blowing open,
nice tablecloths, high class space,
sides of meat, streaming red, glistening, clotted yellow.

Push the paint, whip it around.
It likes it. A strip-tease

without the tease and without stopping at the skin.
The girl thinks I want to see her body—

surprise! Keep your clothes on, sweetie,

you're here to wave away flies.
They're actually pretty, patchy fur swarming

over the side of beef if you
let them settle, but it's

much prettier bare.
Keep waving.

Your arms are killing you? So what.
After four days hanging there it doesn't
smell so great?

Hey, my blood didn't taste so great
when the god-fearing neighbors beat me up

in the name of the almighty.
Thou shalt make no graven images

and thou shalt smash the kid
who tries to paint the rabbi

and here's one for free
in case anybody forgets what No means.

3

Let's build a frame of common
sense, stating the case with deeply

received ideas and fields of trophies
to hold the still-warm ashes, yes?

What's happening? Soutine, non-verbal painter
of crooked landscapes, people, meat, is speaking,

supposedly, but it can't be, time
is a problem, and place,

one's place in the senses, facts of habit, recognition,
situations where art is produced, carefully broken windows

placed at careful distances
from customers who are always right.

The dramatic monolog is far down on the list
of living forms, supine, disgusting really.

What is an anecdotal Soutine to me,
and what am I to these

acidic bursts of no one's speech

and they to the decomposing composition?
The desire for heroic writing splits

into appetite (glug glug!) and horror
at the achieved sentence (keep waving!),

while the eye (your mind or
mine?) sticks the words like pigs,

with syntax underneath to catch the
flows of meaning. The taste

of lost things is a tyrannical pleasure
and is always in infinite supply.

4

For the sake of art,
modernist coffee, Paris,

it would be nice
to hold some things separate,

let the anxious animal graze outside forever
on museum grass

while, inside, history's waterfall flows upward,
sharp white walls

keeping the vision of taste safe
from the mouth that wants grapes

perpetually bursting into the old original wine:
Make It New.

The Louvre
is the *shtetl* of *shtetls*.

Unless our home
is language, raising us

inside its womb. Reading its shifting glitter
I almost forget I ever learned

to write in half-lit
rooms and blocks and days.
There are lives outside

the correction chambers of this page.
Couldn't it be stronger? Time

to stop and name. Print
on paper for the neighbors.

## THE HEROES

Never turn down
what the gods
give. What gods?
Eyes see out.
Or you can argue.

Those people are dead.
Their money's gone.
Hammer-shaped clouds.
Like, kind, paired eyes
blink, shut, close.

Is poetry's
power utterly
unlegislatable? Are there
holes in my head?
I ape my body.

Could this be
exactly not?
The key turns
its letters.
Tongue through the door.

Change the way
the tape
talks. Sweep up
while the weather
moves.

The story rules
the past.
Bend the bars
with puny words.
Back and forth.

Achilles shakes
his tiny spear,
his will a dot,
a dime. Phone's
still connected.

Go home to
your wife, Odysseus,
goat, bear, name
fitting neatly
in the meter.

The line breaks
in two.
Long dark purple waves
cover themselves
with glory.

A mountainous litany
where they died.
The insanity, sing,
goddess, of the son
of the father,

destruction,
psyches blown flat
to hell, human
birdseed, executing
god's orders, start

anywhere. Crash forward
to undone thought.
The river rises
and talks, a
horse comments.

The man, to me,
intone, muse,
polyvalent, the one
who, very much,
trying, wandered, hurt.

Home and war
are absolute categories.
Touch the monster, you die.
Who can see
around the block?

I'll lash myself
to my ear, pulse
pounding autonomous,
untranslatable,
irresistible.

Behavior only looks
understandable
from a place
without self-interest.
I don't follow.

They're killing
each other down
there. The plot's
cross-purposed. No one
forgets a word.

Long ago, sitting
on a coarse beach,
eating animals.
Spoils.
Just noise.

The names repel
everything else.
No one could ever quite
live there.
Wishes pound words.

Speech lets
noise fall down
off them, they
go, they're gone.
They lost.

# THE MANCHURIAN CANDIDATE: A REMAKE

1st shot (for the trailer)

Bang we see the crosshairs targeting
the spineless forehead

2nd shot

Didn't you hear me the first time?
We know you know what we're saying to you.

3rd shot

They have such power over me
but Frank isn't bothered by them all that much.

*Ulysses* lies there on his floor
a closed block with a big name.

4th shot

Closeup of the dustjacket: words.
They have power over me.

The dustjacket is orange and black
but this is black and white so I just say it.

The cover isn't part of the book—obviously.
I'm not in the movie—obviously.

5th shot (for the trailer)

A harpsichord on the soundtrack signals
something's false—this is the 50s remember.

On top they're hearty, fussy old ladies;
underneath they're murderous cold war hypnotists.

On top they're discussing hydrangeas; underneath
they make soldiers strangle each other.

On top it's a movie;
on top the frozen war.

Underneath markets wither; underneath
pleasure, all its eggs in one basket, explodes at the sound of shots.

Underneath you have to follow these words to the letter.
You're on top.

### 6th shot

At last the truth can be told.
Let all the spies stand naked.

I was sitting in the den
watching a tape of *The Manchurian Candidate*,

secular, married, legible, American,
looking at what's showing.

Let all the words be sold at cost.
Let all the words be read at cost.

I was playing solitaire because of Korea.
The deck contained 52 diamond queens.

### 7th shot

That was in the movie,
but a picture is exactly where I don't want to live.

PANDA—Where would you like to live? China?

KOALA—I'd love to visit. The food, the umbrellas, the bicycles. Where would you like to live? Australia?

PANDA—Australia's too ironic for my taste. I'd love to visit, though. I've never seen a kangaroo. Their leg muscles must be remarkable.

It looked as if I was coming out ahead.
Not quite victory, perhaps,

but what have we been fighting for
all our lives if not

a New York
where you can go into a bar in the fifties,

order a beer and read *Ulysses*?

I saw paradise the other night.
It was as easy to read as breathing
and writing one's invitation to the world
in progress, frank, surprised, very amused.

It was a dream I can't remember
—obviously—in a phrase not this one:

this is just an assertive shielding
echo, a deeply loved surface.

Then I woke up. I was watching television.

8th shot

The clicker and a right hand above grey couch material.

23

9th shot

The grey voice never transgressing word boundaries,
the plate compartmentalized, the carrot section

filled precisely, never a spatter of pureed orange
slopping into the section for desire,

which was filled with a clear layer
of deeply loved picture:

the blonde biking by tearing off her blouse to bandage his leg
where the snake had conveniently just sunk his admittedly
        abstract, offscreen fangs

—Why not? narrative homeruns
over the abyss of incoherence

are America's
ice cream—

I saw leaden geo-toy Raymond Shaw
murder mother and father
in the snap of the plot;

10th shot

while I was waiting for the kids to go to sleep
so you could nicely slip your underwear off.

Oops you went to sleep.
I never meant any of this.

I have not done these things. Any of these things.
I write for you and strangers.

24

11th shot

in her bra, outside. Summer.
Some are others.

Not her.
Friendly. Filmy.

12th shot

I place myself in the position of the viewer, then I view.
On the night in question I was home all evening, viewing.

13th shot

Frank Sinatra's had it. The social cardboard's
not worth the sweat he constantly carries around on his face.

Wherever he looks:
locked American lives.

No writing the great book.
Might as well read the ashtray.

No loving the great smile, no riding
the city down to bodies

that can be yours for the right song,
the instant aria just before the light changes.

Too many cigarettes,
too many buddies strangling each other.

Why? Because.
Why? Because the smiling Chinese totalizing science sentencer
    of history

pronounced the words, just the pleasantest trace of accent,
"With the hands."

14th shot (for the trailer)

I Chinese view duty-free writing strangle experience
you Amerikanski mister irony door plenty WD-40 but no key
    poly-sci thinker figure out later-never.

15th shot

Frank wasn't strangled but now he can't read *Ulysses*.
It means nothing to him, just another big brick of paper named
    after itself.

When the world is weird,
being bounced around on a word trampoline won't get you any rest.

From in front of the VCR field in the psychic past of the Cold War,
this is Bob Perelman.

16th shot

Yes, mother, every word must count: 6
Yes, father, I will count each word: 7

If any one of them gets away
then I will be alone in

a locked mess. The warm curves
the grassy hills and the actual caves

I will want to write myself.
Please I'll write it myself.

The way the streets look from inside the house,
at night, either end blocked or shielded,

the maple leaves lit black green
by streetlights, stating my feelings of home,

mouth and ear and leading them
out to the attentive spark. I read

Jack Kerouac who is free
to drive a Ford in the specific direction

of heaven where art
is a very good investment,

although you only should say that
well after the fact.

In 1955 the many love the few
or at least the few are free to think that they do

and "it was a very good year,"
the present recording its pleasure in being

recorded. Frank Sinatra is rewarded
with a stage full of panties and keys

while standing up and swaying,
his inward light spotlit smokily,
throat open to extort
every sung syllable,
the bedroom board meeting
smoldering, shareholders on fire,
humming along. In 1955, art is
as exciting as the perfect bid,
the sunsoaked homerun,
the victory over the others
that they like too, acknowledge, buy,
put on the wall.

Kids wait,
but the early offscreen doors don't reopen.

17th shot (voiceover)

*The Manchurian Candidate* stars Frank Sinatra
as Benny Marco, Lawrence Harvey as

the horrible Raymond Shaw, Janet Leigh
as Benny's girlfriend, Angela Lansbury as

Shaw's mastermind mother. American soldiers are
betrayed in Korea, and captured by

the Chinese Communists. After offscreen brainwashing,
they are shown to the Russians.

Both groups are intellectuals, quoting conflicting
studies as the commonsense Americans sit,

bored but patient, in alternate shots,
brainwashed into thinking they're at a

horticultural meeting in New Jersey where
matrons in white dresses and broad

flowery hats are attending a lecture
extolling scientific gardening. "Another modern discovery

which we owe to the hydrangea
concerns the influence of air drainage

upon plant climate." Slow modern harpsichord
jangles the soundtrack. The film is

racially progressive: when the onscreen American
soldier is black, his hallucinated matrons

are uppermiddleclass black; there's no plantation
subtext. When Shaw is ordered to

strangle another soldier, he's almost too
polite, saying "Excuse me" as he

brushes another's chair; the soldier to
be strangled is polite, too. It's

a liberal utopia: good manners have
triumphed over competition. The Chinese are

jovial and authoritative—they've perfected the
procedure. They can make the Americans

believe anything: the Camels they're smoking
turn out to be yak dung.

It is to laugh, for the
Chinese mastermind at least. The Russians

are surly and badly in need
of dental work. You can't believe

what you see. But you have
to look. Finally, the poem is

beginning to focus. We know you
know what we're saying to you.

KOALA—I hit my head; I had a dream. Isn't that how it always
starts?

PANDA—Maybe that's the way it starts in the West. It's not a collec-
tive form; there's no rhetorical place for people to come together.
That's the way you've started, but that's not the way it's supposed to
start. Hitting your head is personal.

KOALA—I was cutting the grass and I hit my head on the branch of an apple tree. An old one, twenty-five feet tall with two live quarters sprouting north and south, two dead ones east and west. It was not symbolism, only matter. If you don't believe me, you can feel the ridge of healing flesh on my head, under the fur here. It's as real as history.

PANDA—Cutting the grass is a fairly trivial instance upon which to balance the non-concentric circles of history. Go in, I would have said, have a little lemonade, & read Whitman or the Misty poets. Particulars only exist by being collective.

KOALA—So the public—fuzzy little me in the case of your remarks—becomes crucial.

PANDA—When you're a nation, being cute is not enough any more. No, a public is a serious, collective enterprise. The ironic single writer in a cage, treasonous, or loyal, or mad, riven by pathos, unfamiliar tears . . . it doesn't really matter much to the words or the world. Once the hypnosis of the singular is snapped, that is. Before, one can think that anything might happen on the page.

KOALA—I'm willing to bob for very small favors, balls of hard, candied poetry swimming almost ethically in the sweat of irony's personal furnace around which individuals are gathered into gendered masses in lieu of lives for all lived under the changeable blue fields of utopia otherwise known as international justice!

PANDA—International justice! I think we might as well change the subject, don't you?

KOALA—Fine. Which do you hate more, symbolic poetry, or poetry that's all language?

PANDA—Easy: poetry that's symbolic.

KOALA—But what about poetry that's all language?

30

PANDA—Poetry that's all language makes me cry when I'm asleep and can't hear the tears hitting the pillow, I mean the page.

KOALA—I actually hit my head: that means something. It was hot, I was one body for the duration, cutting the leaves of grass and I saw myself walking on air on cloud stilts of biological perpetuity and sweat of the word. I was not a nation, I was not a species, I was a speaker, fully alive just because I like the sound of that the noisome hiss of this making a made world under me undergo twisting birth and destruction just to keep me saying what I was going to say anyway! Or anything else! Or nothing so what black hole blank! An apple an unoriginal rhetorical sin a day goes astray into the many minds of the many many others who don't think this! And neither do I! Neither we nor me! Am I allowed to say this? No! I say it! Thanks to the body beyond species, beyond genre, thanks to the dictionary, the strikers, the Haymarket lexicographers! The Tiananmen Square grammarians! I say it! Out loud! Where was I? Where are we? Don't you love the intrusion of speech where no speech can be, life where sounds are the slippery start to never finish but get there already anyway . . .

PANDA—Did you show that to your trainer before you turned it loose on me?

KOALA—My teacher?

PANDA—I'm assuming your teacher was your trainer before he was your teacher.

18th shot

I can't remember the movie anymore.

Art means throwing scraps of code

to the bodies as appetite supplements.

The screen is softwired so the bars disappear.

31

after the primal shot

I can see eyes painted open
on the death mask of that lovely
arrangement I used to call the world,
America, my life, the page,
the academy of the future,
which, as it turns out,
is in the past. They even move.
They're mine: that was home.

It's plain that there was time
and that it took place
but its quick pleasures are now words
in a language with only scattered survivors.

A single word means nothing.

Or a line without a world.

The present is full of survivors' sentences.
With disoriented conviction and memory
too deep for instrumental speech
swimming sinkingly toward pre-owned futures
hosed down the hyperspace of capital
where freedom spells the rampant logos
turning attractively bemused typefaces and icons
toward the traffic.

Or language it for yourself.
Make your own recipes: ironize,
experiment, write wrong,
but don't forget
the old pleasures:
skies, turkeys, playgrounds.

We know you know.
Meanwhile, one drives,

an open lane a paycheck of sorts,
leading to the autobiography glimpsed
in the gas station john mirror.

During the war there's nothing to eat
but information and denial, the new
mixing with the old
down through all the details. Taste.

19th shot

Who folded my clothes?
You did! I did!

Who watered my tears?
You did! I did!

Who batted an eye each word I woke?
You did! I did!

Who waited for me to sleep so I could wake one step further inside
    the world?
You did! I did!

KOALA—To survive you have to be willing to do anything.
Anthologies! That's where the money really is, or might be. At least
so I imagine from my fuzzy animal distance. Reprint the material!
Dominate the gene pool! Rise like Godzilla and make them read
you for fucking ever!

PANDA—If you use language like that, you'll have a hard time
even making it into the La Brea tar pits.

20th shot

To be free and to be
Frank Sinatra the pinnacle artist

33

but to be pictured as *homo ordinarius*
keeping the public world private

by visible quotidian heroism:
that's the lesson scorching the director's desire

in every shot. If you feel like arguing
with the movies, then step outside.

21st shot

The Chinese mastermind has the one
successful marriage in the movie.
(Yes, it's offscreen: you can't have everything.)

He's really a most happy fella.

We rejoin him as he leaves
the Russian doctor-spy's so-called clinic in NYC
after ordering Shaw to murder
his would-have-been father-in-law, the honest muckraking journalist,
as well as the love-of-his-life blonde.
Don't fall asleep,
this is plot.
Everyone has to sacrifice.

Except for the mastermind perhaps,
jauntily tugging his gloves tight,
saying now he has to get off to Macy's
for some Xmas shopping.
Smiles the happy social smile sans dissonance:
the wife gave him a list yea long,
shrugs: what are you gonna do?

He knows how to get in bed with capital
and let it charm his pants off.
Having them "tight enough

so everyone will want to go to bed with you,"
as Frank O'Hara writes, is a youthful gesture
under the dappled shade of capital's
frond-like pleasances.

That's one thing.
But to live as a large system of control is quite another.

As the mastermind leaves, the Russian stares.
He just doesn't get it:
he believes in history
not Macy's, inexorable direction, totality,
the concrete-translucent materiality of class to classless truth,
one world one history at the end!

Meanwhile one's provisional oneness
stands and waits with oblique conviction
against the waterfall of wage-slaves
—that rainbow spray is guilty as Sunday!
Those sunny lakes, those caves of ice,
those miracles of rare device
forced from the deep romantic chasm
of bourgeois pastoral-pornographic shopping,
which that crypto-individualist Chinese mastermind indulges
with his credit flowing past the respectful cashier
like vodka down a mule's throat!
Or whatever!

Thus the Russian revolutionary-bureaucrat-murderer-actor
placed on the verbal screen
by the all-too-human history of this shot.

              closing shot

Shaw's gunsight targets
Communist McCarthyite foster father's forehead,

as said before, though in a novel continuum.

The movie wants to reach the new world
and, in the same gesture,

to conclude. A narrative should hold you
with intimate concern, but not too close

because you'll be heading out one day,
pegged, looking back

for the recognizable trees, the known cars,
glad animal movements traded in
for manageable novelty . . .

Is the nostalgia for creation or destruction,
or for something that hasn't happened yet?

Beside the encrusted place names,
flags of private longing
flutter against the vistas,
and molecular revolutionaries dream of taking all desires to court
and setting them loose beneath the robes of judgment.

To pull the gown from knowledge,
to pull the eye from noon,
and not to see the catered wants
of Tom, Dick, and Harry
navigating the street, the mall, the clicker and the dust!

And Jane, Ketisha, and those tender technocratic shoots and stumps,
you and me?

On screen, nations personify the pursuit of happiness,
tearing families to shreds and the shreds
to costumed certainties of  loss and rage.
Beyond the blinds:
the end—rain falling on cue,
Frank Sinatra crying, Janet Leigh wordless.

The days regular as sprocket holes,
while decades slide by
with unevenly layered minds of their own.

You! Hypocrite viewer! With nothing but mirrors
for pleasure, knowledge, luck.
My hand in yours if you read me.
Those deprogrammed people glimmering beyond
the evening's blocky conspiracy theories,
willing their present without shooting our past
to a bloody parable
—have you found a way to call them yet?

## THE ILIAD, CONTINUED

1.
So that
was that,

leaving a land
of language and slave
economics, literature
and other delayed

explosions, grecian
formula columns crouching below
budget ceilings, on which
maps of free play

transected by the Styx
the O-hi-o or
whatever the local water
so long as it flowed.

2.
No more
blind storylines,

let the current
rivers go about their
business speechlessly,
as well they

should, since
postwar words are, one
would think, capable of
spotting the systematically big

stick and random stigmata
speckling the winning
cities and looted populations
The page is no one's.

[*Iliad*, Book 21: When Achilles dumps too many bodies into the Skamander, the river tells him to stop.]

## TO THE FUTURE

I always expected some kind of
indefinite continuance but it turns out

my body was smaller and more
attached to its beginnings than I

thought. So the world will end
up breaking apart. No surprise there,

really, though I'll probably feel a
bit shocked all the way through:

familiarity has its charm, as real
as sex, and it's a lot

more spread out. I'll jot down
some lasting impressions—sorry—last impressions.

Last night I caught a fragile
glimpse of the writing surface of

dreams: it was like a sheet
of water I could feel as

an edge my body interrupted; I
was in a pool, sticking out,

and when I wanted anything, felt
desire as the words say then

the edge would disappear—it would
be the same temperature as me and

I'd find myself back in the
story. Which was? Something about getting

published. There was a tall building,
downtown San Francisco where they assembled

flyers to be distributed in laundromats.
These were frequented by large immigrant

populations as well as disgruntled aristocrats
back from the ex-colonies. Then I

was in the laundromat, naked, washing
the books I managed to save

from the war. These were quite
sturdy, as you might imagine. The

sex practices of the sixties, set
to music by Marianne Moore and

Jimi Hendrix. People would study these,
as well as other power sources:

wind, sun, linebreaks. Once a page
would get clean enough then I

could write on top of it.
Like now: fake dreams, skittish prophecy—

it doesn't matter as long as
the breath comes a little quicker,

and the pulse firms and skips:
not too much: the door between

centuries turns out to be quite
narrow. An Egyptian Pulled Glass Bottle

in the Shape of a Fish;
Six Words to Name a Nipple.

My heart's pounding a bit: it
must be the future. So long.

# FAKE DREAMS

## THE POPE

January 19: No contact this morning.
The Pope and I were going

to have lunch at what he
said would be "The Waldorf." We

walked there through a somewhat subaqueous
New York: sweating walls, women in

Hawaiian shirts, men in aprons with
beads of perspiration on their cheeks.

Suggestion of mold everywhere, most surfaces
carrying hints of blue, green, silver.

Some low lintels even had seaweed.
The Pope was wearing his full

outfit: his miter of course made
him look quite tall and his

robes puffed him out sideways too.
I asked him how he was

handling the humidity. He said it
was all Gore-tex, gesturing toward his

robes as we strode along. We
laughed. But I didn't hear the

swishing sound Gore-tex makes: his clothes
were quiet. We got to "the

Waldorf," which was a Greek place,
the "W'orf." It really was something

of a wharf. We sat at
a table made from a large

wooden spool, the kind for holding
miles of phone wire. The ceiling

was low, decorated with fishing net
and red and green colored lights.

We looked out at some dark
view that had water in it.

He ordered fried calamari and so
did I. So now the time

had come. "What about Jesus Christ?"
I asked him. "He's supposed to

have come down from heaven, and
I'm not interested?" The Pope finished

squeezing a wedge of lemon onto
his sandy curlicues. He kept looking

at what he was doing as
he spoke, although in fact he

had finished doing it. "The file
cabinets were ordered a long time

ago. They thought they were very
big at that time. Nobody's allowed

to look in them, anyway. Look,
I'm enjoying my squid. How's yours?"

Yes, mine was pretty good too.
I noticed his English was unaccented.

How come no hint of Polish?
"I'm universal," he said. We laughed.


## THE AVANT-GARDE

January 17: Nothing. Scraps. Can't remember.

I was marching in the avant-garde
army. We were on a dirt

road leading to Trenton. It was
sunny, well-tended farms, beets doing well,

tomatoes, peppers, and we had momentum.
The occasional Model-T pulled off to

the side to let us by.
People were wearing more or less

what I'd read about. The Baroness
was wearing purple metal; her breasts

were aggressively festooned. Pound wore a
brown suit; tall and dowdy, he

joked that he was president of
Ohio State. He took some buckeyes

from his pocket: "You can't eat
em, but you can't beat em."

He closed them tightly in his
fist at the punchline; I heard

him repeat the routine. Eliot wore
a kind of lederhosen jogging suit:

shorts and suspenders but made out
of soft grey shoddy. In fact

his suspenders broke, as one could
easily have predicted. He stopped, shamefaced

as his chestnut leather undershorts were
revealed. He fell out and began

doing fast continuous pushups. He was
short and quite strong. He pistoned

with a cartoon intensity which, it
became clearer with every stroke, wasn't

going to go away. We left
him there. Marianne Moore wore a

long white gown with a dildo
tucked in a slot right above

her buttocks. No, it was a
tight scroll, which she could unroll

and read, although only a few
words at a time, as they

were highly acidic. She had a
short haircut, walked fast & happily.

The skirt-material was canvas, she thrashed
it from inside, it billowed. She

was sailing. I was next to
the Baroness. She turned to me,

playfully but intently rubbed some metal
on her breast against my arm.

It was hard to keep the
sense of tableau from sliding: we

were walking forward at some clip.
She said this was my "inoculation."

She laughed, revealing a gaptoothed mouth,
problems: brown teeth, purple gentian stain.

Then she sucked my arm: "To
compose you." She had a whistle

hanging between her breasts. She took
it, blew hard: some people came

with a wide litter: "Come on,"
she said, while we all continued

marching forward, "You need to get
particular." She hopped up weightlessly. Dreams

are more unfair to the dreamer
than to the dreamed, I thought,

heaving myself up after her. Once
I was up there, she looked

at me sharply: "You think this
is the avant-garde? You don't know

where the edges are. Where do
you think these guys are heading?

Trenton! 'Trenton Makes and the World
Takes!' The avant-garde? Professionalization! Reviewing!
   Reproduction!

Look. See the wisps? Khlebnikov is
burning his last book. He's not

in the army. There. In the
middle of the cabbage. What a

bad dad." She laughed. "He's set
his beard on fire this time!"

Fake. False. Faux. For the archive.


## THE LIBRARY

January 28: We were going to
have sex in the stacks. We

were in the 800's, standing eagerly
amid the old copies of the

Romantics. Looking at the dark blue
spines of Wordsworth's *Collected*, I thought

47

how the intensity of his need
to express his unplaced social being

in sentences had produced publicly verifiable
beauty so that his subsequent civic

aspirations seemed to have importance enough
for him to become Poet Laureate

and how his later leaden writing
upheld that intensity and verifiability, only

instead of searching wind and rocks
and retina for the sentences of

his social being, he chirped his
confirmed lofty perch to other social

beings in lengthy claustrophobic hallelujahs for
the present moment. There are devices

to keep it still, long enough,
and he had learned them. Rhyme

was a burden, crime was unambiguously,
explainably wrong, time had snuck around

behind him. He had carved his
own anxiety into a throne and

now he was stuck on it,
remembering sadder days when he had

wanted to be happy with a
purity that made him blink, thinking

back. He remembered in a trance:
the past seemed unbearably near. Our

more slippery, contrapuntal hallelujahs were planted
in the immediate future, only a

few buttons, zippers and a little
elastic down the road. We had

first snuck into the men's room
but it had been crowded with

two intensely separated men hunched at
urinals 1 and 6. We turned

to hurry out, and you pointed
to the magic marker graffiti on

the beige tiles: "This place needs
a women's touch" answered by "FINGER

MY ASSHOLE, CUNT!" This second message
had been modified by an arrow

indicating "CUNT" was to be moved
from behind to before "ASSHOLE": "FINGER

MY CUNT, ASSHOLE!" We were eager
to prove syntax was not mere

vanity and that bodies could use
it to resist the tyranny of

elemental words. And wouldn't it be
nice to get knowledge and pleasure

on the same page. So we'd
hurried out to the deserted 800's.


## THE GAME

February 24: Yesterday there was weather;
tomorrow there will be none. I'm

in an academic office, surrounded by
screens, each with a keyboard attached.

The screens depict scenes in cities;
I'm to type in words. I

type "PLAY" and a section in
the southeast of one city blows

up: a seven-story parking structure and
a big boxy sewage treatment facility

with its attendant pond goes boom:
a grainy spray of particles expands

up in a vee and then
falls while the sound system produces

a sharp burst of static until
the particles have vanished, leaving a

tan crater. "GUILT," on the other
hand, creates a whole flat small

town on a screen which had
shown 'verdant' forest. I see a

little car moving down "Main Street."
It stops and makes a right.

I go over to a third
screen with a generic New York

City and type "I LIKE HORSES"
but nothing happens. "I GET OFF

ON THE HORSES OF INSTRUCTION THE
HELL WITH THE MARLBORO MAN": still

nothing. Apparently syntax cancels out the
effects. Okay, so just plain "HORSES."

Anything? Yes, a tiny pup tent
has appeared in the lower righthand

corner, on the sidewalk in front
of a department store. I try

"I": a second pup tent. "LIKE":
a third. The power of writing

in this particular game is starting
to feel, shall we say, illusory.

An authority (dressed in blue) is
in the doorway with three large

yellow envelopes. He is holding them
out to me; none have return

addresses and the authority is both
offering and withholding them. It is

mail/not-mail (perhaps one is a letter
bomb). I can see the address

on the top envelope—it was
written with a sweeping gesture by

someone using a two-tone (red and
silver) pen and shows great flourish,

I know from this that the
top envelope contains a literary magazine.

Suddenly I feel deeply vexed; tears
start, though I hold them, and

I feel dizzy. I don't know
about the other two envelopes. I

don't take them. I gesture toward
the screens. "You take a turn,"

I say. But he pauses, "a
turn" doesn't compute. He seems to

feel the screens and keyboards are
a site fraught with dignity and

heroic challenge. I offer him a
cigarette. He takes it with earnest

gratefulness. As I offer the match
he's in bureaucratic heaven inhaling with

rapt concentration. I drop the pack
to the floor, squash it, rubbing

it heavily with the ball of
my foot until tobacco and paper

are spread. Tears are flowing down
my cheeks. He's smoking, wide-eyed, silent.

Soon I'm standing on the grass
near home, which is set amid

an array of terraced gardens. Other
people are there, including T. Three

times in quick succession a terrific
thunderous roar fills the air and

the ground rumbles and shakes. We
all know then that hundreds of

miles away great monsters have emerged
from the ground. They are reptilian

but insect-like, giant ants with nimble
alligator limbs. It is comforting to

know they are "hundreds, maybe thousands"
of miles away, but eventually they

will come; it's common knowledge that
they particularly hate poets. Their most

fearsome posture is when they arrange
themselves into words. They can get

us at a distance that way.
We talk nervously, trying to inhabit

our seconds with the timbres of
our voices; we make long sentences;

we gesture and laugh as accurately
as we can. Timing is crucial.

[with Lyn Hejinian]


VICTORY

December 25: I was at Putney,
it was beautiful.

Reuben was graduating,
this was the end of my close involvement.

Francie was on one side,
Chloe Deal on the other.

Do you need another woman in your twosome,
I'd volunteer.

Not consequential,
dream kept unrolling.

I went over to George Iffington with the tortoise shell glasses and
    plastic hair,
he mumbled.

He was full of literary talk,
did he know who I was?

Brecht would write a play, he dismissed,
then a novel.

Never stuck with anything,
that was his problem.

I leaned up close,
heard nothing but class.

Then Robert Lowell drove into the diningroom in his stretch limo,
Iffington got in as Lowell ranted.

"*Can* you write better than Sid
Kunitz, Bob Berryman? That's the only

question it makes any sense to
stammer back to." He swerved sharply

to avoid a buffet table, but
didn't quite make it. A tailfin

hurled a tray of cold cuts
to the floor. "The answer is

you, manic, self-born, self-deceased, performing for
also-dead papa, stuck up over the

stage like a lead eagle, eyes
welded shut to render judgment all

the more unanswerable. So you dance
to that blindness, type your flintlock

accuracies into that stone page. If
you dislike those odds, long as

a loser's memory, then face backwards
and wait for the future to

commence. Don't blink, you'll spoil. Meanwhile
the missiles bristle like red, white

and blue thistles, or the Cold
War's over, isn't it? Mine is.

I'm overexposed now, with critics crawling
between my lines. Get a life,

then get it over with! Follow
me, you bad singularities, worse infinities!

If you want a career, die!"
The car nosed significantly against the

wall and he backed up, leaving
a silver smear on the splintered

pine boards. The left headlight was
smashed. "1946, 1966, the pricks stuck

a crown on a head that
was barely mine. The wavering ceilings

of home! And so I was
elected king of poetry and lived

more or less ever after in
the castle where they manufacture awards

without labor, far down in the
upper middle reaches. It's all done

by Santa's literary elves with their
mirror-powered pleasure-centers and delicate feeding tubes,

pressing the bar, spreading the word,
North Pole on south, Satan's auratic

face on the dust-covers. Dust to
dust for the industrious poets. Microbes

of culture carbuncling the prairie that
knows no trough above the nightly

news. My native massacres! All for
a few dozen home runs, a

few hundred creamy hotels. That's not
all I wanted. I'm not boring

you by any chance? Dead men's
rants are the worst, stuck in

traffic, suing the dictionary." By now
the diners were up and shouting

as he zigzagged rapidly. He hipchecked
one, who flew sideways, and then

caught another flush in the back,
dragging him under the front wheels.

"I myself am fame, hard, gemlike.
Or was. Mention me outside, if

there still is one. The cock
is crowing and the reviewless dawn

begins to glare. Here, take the
wheel. Islington? Stifflington? —No license? Anxiety's

our golden rule, our sublimated sublime.
It's cheating: that's how you play."


## CHOCOLATE

December 2: Nick and Nora were in Hershey
for their honeymoon; they even toured

the chocolate factory the first afternoon.
Of course there were martinis before

and smoke after sex, like the
movies said. Her cigarettes and his

cigars re-asserted personal Alleghenies of taste
under the omnipresent smell of chocolate.

The putative 3-D of the thin
clouds was an almost satisfying picture

of the unpredictable organizations of imagination.
And then the taste, the ash

of the usual wants, making their
tongues a touch ugly and articulate

in the midst of desire, stirring
the whole kettle, at least a

layer or so down. But pleasure
was much bigger than their bodies,

and, after they had had their
particular fill, they began to notice

the chocolate air again. They lay
back and stared up at the

off-white silk of the canopy. Tasks
lay ahead, inert, scattered, and the

more they thought about them, the
more urgent. "You know, there's Kingston

in San Fran, and Hughes in
Harlem. They're not getting any clearer."

"Train schedule?" "In my jacket." Nick
gestured over toward the ornamental desk

the hotel provided. He fell back
and sighed. "Chocolate. Think you'll ever

be able to stand it again?"
"Yeah." "Yeah, huh?" "'Yeah': you're very

perceptive." Nora reached for a bar
on the bedside table, opened it,

and broke off a piece. She
put it to his lips, pushed

herself onto him to free her
other hand, which she used to

open his mouth. He resisted, but
she edged a thumb and forefinger

in and stretched insistently. When it
was open enough she laid the

square of chocolate on his tongue.
"Feeding time." Then she closed his

lips, pinching them and sliding them
back and forth across each other.

"See. It's good." She watched his
tongue moving inside and grinned when

she saw him swallow. He answered
through compressed lips, "Yeah, it's good."

## IN A NUTSHELL

Credo in a kind of American Jewish Hamlet-like
bagel, a bit round for action yet leavened
enough by contact with the near live past
—you call it landscape, I call it history—
to provide a layered vantage. Round yet curiously
unconscious in the center as if problems with
royal parentage might be dissolved by fanatic attention
to license plate coincidence. Heart beats, mind floods,

whose news is this? Turn, turn again, spread
a minimum of cream cheese, feed desire its
networks. A you for all the secrets. But
if I have to vote, edge, root, fax
& already feel, as opposed to an unrehearsed
life, well, slide over a few inches &
we'll make room for each other's public. Not
the heresy of paraphrase, not the hearsay of

phrase, but a general agreement to differ from ourselves.

## TO THE PAST

Take down my books, mother,
the song says and I see
rain streak the sacred tablets,
graffiti between music and speech.

Take them down,
for I am alive today
my body an example,
the computer a black tray,

semiautomatic code behind the plastic
spraying a lichenlike display,
autonomous wash of power
down the drain, prismatic, pissed away

to ease the painful suture
where tip of tongue
meets tip of iceberg,
language melting in its future.

Before I could read,
I heard you with as much belief
as any made
thing in the snowy heights

pursuing the self, apelike, alplike
—I mean, let the pines do
what they want, squirrels leap, clouds work on their memoirs all day:
still, I'll never undo

the stitches of artificial life. And I hear
something similar happened to you
and to your you
and to her

before that, all the way
back to the history bogs where stenographers
lie frozen in writing degree zero.
Take them all down, they won't stay put anyway.

In some other poem
you wiggle your can
crazily, signifying America
for William Carlos Williams making music

in a gender
desert. Modernism's big adventure
is still in print
on matchbooks and corporate towers,

an education in management distances
holding mirrors up
to men in cars,
women floodlit in anorexic bowers

with customers paying for the pleasure
of buying. Meaning is a dog,
following masters, scratching after hours
in the local doghouse,

a mea culpa inside each command,
flash floods leaving the syntax damp,
pliable, but the dead
resistant as sand.

For now, motion
is still modern,
automatic, riding flindered wills
past each moment.

## RELIGION IN THE REGIONS OF MATTER

I'm Jewish. The sky is pink.
The words are written. Respect the materials.

End of poem.

The body in pain, the body in panic, the body in court of law, the body under the wheel of the sentence, the body flying on the sound of the line as it hits.

There's enough shampoo for tomorrow & enough milk for breakfast, the only problem, really, is tone and direction.

The sky is grey.

As grey as if having written it once means writing it always.

There's the original audience: imaginary, improbable as an ever-fixèd mark, and what to say to that? tugging at the anchor in the dark messing up the stars on the water. Don't call it "information": the screen's too undulant for generations to know each other's names except as nagging contracts, life and contacts. Thanks, Echo, tanks. Words sound. Who knew, except for you? Puppy tail, Talmud trail. Are you Jewish? I'm Jewish.

Don't worry, I'll revise, I'll see the sky again, sober as a historian at a graveside desk.

Turn over, lovely trout, and let me fry your other side.

You smell delicious, and if love is a metaphor,
then food is an allegory of this very world

—you know, the one with bones in it,
and an appetite for time, and bodies like ourselves.

## WRITING IN REAL TIME

Real time, lived experience:
sixteen thousand four hundred and thirty eight.

Aren't you the real life of adjectives?
Sixteen thousand four hundred and thirty nine.

Real, lived, gong-tormented,
sixteen thousand four hundred and forty,
you have begun writing a poem:
sixteen thousand four hundred and forty one.

One can be Pound,
take a short walk on a long pier,
reading books on microbes,
scratching wrists raw,
thinking at racial & aesthetic purity,
or not,
sixteen thousand four hundred and forty two.

Imagine sixteen thousand four hundred and forty three,
the stars and the stripes forever,
blue sky on a 29-cent stamp,
sixteen thousand four hundred and forty four.

My cap is on—San Diego Chargers—my life is gone.
Sixteen thousand four hundred and forty five,
sixteen thousand four hundred and forty six,
sixteen thousand four hundred and forty seven,
sixteen thousand four hundred and forty eight,
sixteen thousand four hundred and forty nine.

Turn the Washington Monument into a maypole.
Humanize reason, nation.

Sing sixteen thousand four hundred and fifty
and the plangent quartertone just above,
underdone, twinged down at dark 10:00 A.M.
beside the canal with a heron highstepping
in curiosity sans irony toward some garbage.

You can adjust to the demands,
can you not, knight-at-arms,
alone & palely counting the red sumac leaf,
falling once, through still air,
sixteen thousand four hundred and fifty one.

Not that these demands must come to consciousness,
better that they are consciousness itself,
not your or myself,
the demand to write to see complete
sixteen thousand four hundred and fifty two,
and not be those other ones,
decades ago, wrapped in slaughter,
glamor, gemütlich verbal vacuum
of the known name some other time.

The world, once behind me,
is now all before me,
though not exactly for me.
The world is exact.
These words are exact.
Only sixteen thousand four hundred and fifty three
is inexact, itself,
deformed rain of every, next.

This is the same poem,
the one poem,
the sole aesthetic object,
thrown down and broken open by its rules.

The puppy leaps up,
hoarse, cowed, needy, grateful,

springing out of zero,
you, yours, it's *you,*
*sixteen thousand four hundred and fifty four,*
*your smell, your cheese biscuits.*
The puppy leaps, the entertainment god
smiles at entertainment, the President helicopters
—these are some of the different faces of the same moment
to which we assign the number
sixteen thousand four hundred and fifty five
sixteen thousand four hundred and fifty six
sixteen thousand four hundred and fifty seven
sixteen thousand four hundred and fifty eight
and sixteen thousand four hundred and fifty nine.

I've changed my mind.
In theory, it's enough to think.
In practice, the woman wiping the stony black plastic tables
at the Science Museum restaurant
has two hours and twenty minutes to go she told me.

Sixteen thousand four hundred and sixty
sixteen thousand four hundred and sixty one.
Does that man beat that woman or just read the paper?

It's too late to retrace half thoughts.
They sounded intriguing, but are written
sixteen thousand four hundred and sixty two.

What a triumph it would be to get to 17,000.
I've thought that more than once
the last few months,
though never in that form,
never using the word 'triumph'
or the construction 'What a . . .'

Triumph of the will to lunch
& kill the world to praise the name
sixteen thousand four hundred and

67

turn back to check verisimilitudinous ink
so close so almost exactly so
with word-to-world marriage
as a sacrament to be placed
in the open reading mouth
watering in a dry month sixty three.

Human the life
the seconds of the same,
human the human
or cease to speak the name,
dogeared sounds spell the golden mean
throughout the greater Philadelphia area,
Louisville proper,
London per se,
the place placed here
to mean to be.

Sensual awakening in even the best books,
short dirty looks,
wife's warm thigh touching just now,
sixteen thousand four hundred and sixty four.

Got a lot of work to catch up on tonight
sixteen thousand four hundred sixty five
sixteen thousand four hundred and sixty six.
And I don't want
to cheat myself
of any of it
sixteen thousand four hundred and sixty seven.

Sixteen thousand four hundred and sixty eight,
I escaped
the once mighty past
the rubble from the best imperial jokes
back to ice caves and earth wobble
& blood-soaked vegetable rituals

vouchsafed to T. S. Eliot & Julia Child,
sixteen thousand four hundred and sixty nine
sixteen thousand

### *LAPTOP*

Here I sit, brokenhearted
producer of American consumption,
lived to write, but
only monitoring the screen.

The exception is now
the only golden rule.
If a body is
a body, then where

in the world is
the World Bank? Right
inside the latest word,
mi palabra su palabra,

speaking subjects
living the exchange rate
every time they open
their single-mouthed dictionary

       four hundred and seventy.
Sixteen thousand four hundred and seventy one.

### LAPTOP (Side B)

Single body single life
is not how
it works. Bushels
rot on docks,

bodies along banks
of pronounceable rivers.
Soft, large, heaped
round numbers form
blurred museums awaiting
the single uncountable
denominator. The founding
fathers guard the
past, a limited
edition of statues
of virtuous activity,
anchoring feelings of
free circulation. Pictures
of bodily wealth
or financial health
almost appear, floating
behind providential malls,
where to park
is to live
the Thanksgiving logic
of a progress
without classes, hoping
for nothing but
the best for
the best. For
the rest, charred
blocks under
frequent
flyer
miles.

Sixteen thousand four hundred and seventy two,
sixteen thousand four hundred and seventy three,
sixteen thousand four hundred and seventy four,

## A PIECE OF PAPER

White wooden rectangle cut and milled smooth to touch as finger slides
along creamy visibility cells locked in sequence supporting the surface
rolling pastoral fields where noon glare makes reading the sun mean sun
blink your blindness inside legibility beating down calls figures of speech

to recline in the empire's massy shade sexy if it comes to that and begging
to be personified used indulged you May it's June and time to say what
you like mouthing your words starting with the lovely body of this one
here on top of the unspoken fibers never commanding a just price

forced to pay homage to the rainbow in the book construed to say I won't
hurt you again violent creation of identity in a sonnet to one's own free
will in the face of immediate wrath bad odds underneath the surface small
room to maneuver up here too where I write in unstable groups of

signifying others who speak and live or not they weren't given air time
and paper to ride this recursive point of entry

sixteen thousand four hundred and seventy five,
sixteen thousand four hundred and seventy six
and sixteen thousand four hundred and seventy seven;
sixteen thousand four hundred and seventy seven
and sixteen thousand four hundred and seventy eight;

## SCHOOL

Here is a fixed picture
of what I learned
the language is a day
taught to be time
and place & night
to lay omnisexed heads
organically named mechanically twined
to test both wills
walking the canonized street
in publically ciphered clothes
to hand one's life
a degree in consumer
senses by sorting instantaneously
through trays of seconds
with judgment learning to
speak as naturally as
a leaf growing to
be a legitimate leaf
and to be green

## COLLEGE

I stands for
identify the subject
of desire on
the one hand

HIV positive driveby
Bosnia positive but
on the other
universal dictator stood
in front of
legibility's cut edge
flanked by urban
heat beneath mythological
dictionaries fallen from
the sky or
pushed one local
leg over the
railing for self-fashioning
the circuits give
no narrative clue
individual solace comes
from eating light
in the movies


## *JOB*

Were you born in one place?
Yes sir in the swamps under

sunlamps in the valley of empiricism
holding veined relics of the old

measures moments spilled for the saga
to gather encrusted gems a life

is a sketch of that life
name over substance Did you die

in one place? Yes sir in
the swamps under sunlamps in the

valley of empiricism holding veined relics
of the old measures moments spilled


sixteen thousand four hundred and seventy nine;
sixteen thousand four hundred and eighty.
These are affects, trance ones
that I don't know
& embrace to feel
sixteen thousand four hundred and eighty one.

I.
Stone washed.
Covering word,
murmur of numerable.
Children of sixteen thousand four hundred and eighty two
—boys will be men
and never themselves without a little
blood in the pudding
sixteen thousand four hundred and eighty three.

I will never be
but mean mean mean
like a heathen down on Keats' knees
praying to sixteen thousand four hundred and eighty four.

There is no cutting short
the significance of placing this word
here and now
as deaths and disasters
finally make dents in taste
sixteen thousand four hundred and eighty five.

Desire itself
sixteen thousand four hundred and eighty six
wanted dead or alive.

Sixteen thousand four hundred and eighty seven.
One must be
absolutely modern and not write
sixteen thousand four hundred and eighty eight.

Sixteen thousand four hundred and eighty nine.
I am writing
what other writers only thought they wrote.
Sixteen thousand four hundred and ninety.

Sixteen thousand four hundred and ninety one.
My life is a complete fragment of yours.
Sixteen thousand four hundred and ninety two
sixteen thousand four hundred and ninety three.

An exploded mall totality shoplifter
yelling at the security guard
caught red-handed enforcing my world
sixteen thousand four hundred and ninety four.

Rather than write out
sixteen thousand four hundred and ninety five
I now want to insert a false memory
of teen sex thees thous shirt & trou
and the cleverness that only wants
to come and be done with itself,
O for a draught of vantage
to be able to name the named
sixteen thousand four hundred and ninety six.

Worth money.
Poem is value.
Sixteen thousand four hundred and ninety seven
sixteen thousand four hundred and ninety eight.

Now more than ever.
Don't wait.
Sixteen thousand four hundred and ninety nine.

1    6    5    0    0
I now see balanced world
1    6    5    0    1
saw was my maiden name
1    6    5    0    2
before I breathed the air
1    6    5    0    3
to see it like nothing.

I & you.
Sixteen thousand five hundred and four.
He & she & it.
Sixteen thousand five hundred and five.
We & you & they
sixteen thousand five hundred and six
& thass that
sixteen thousand five hundred and seven

Lovely transitions
sixteen thousand five hundred and eight
fall apart & flaunt their parts.

Sixteen thousand five hundred and nine.
It's showtime,
dog & pony backwards go time
sixteen thousand five hundred and ten.

He does not know
that he is writing
sixteen thousand five hundred and eleven.
He thinks that
sixteen thousand five hundred and twelve
he is being himself
sixteen thousand five hundred and thirteen.
He places a connecting log in the fire
sixteen thousand five hundred and fourteen.
He feels warm then hot

then cold, stitches showing,
sixteen thousand five hundred and fifteen
and exactly in the middle
sixteen thousand five hundred and sixteen
psychology, or so he thinks.

Sixteen thousand five hundred and seventeen.
Sixteen thousand five hundred and eighteen
sixteen thousand five hundred and nineteen.
Makes a small picture for now.

# LOVE AND PROBABILITY

This probably rhymes
with that. Your
display on the bed
worked on
over years
in our heads
makes that purple
number for instance
something that pulses
through me
faster than
I can say
throb some or
a bit more
and we can
make those
noises we
can't spell. Mine
probably rhymes with
yours. Each time
I hope to
hold the same
different thing,
some residence of
flame, hot
fire, what
to say and
not be tangled
residue of
the words
that died on
the way to
the mall, mad
that the world

hadn't thought
to provide
anything more interesting
than ranked merchandise
because when it
comes time to
say what we
want we want
some live
fucking feeling
turned inside out
so the sun
signifies and we
can use the
light the ancient
hurtling you know
I never
knew you
could do me
up and drop
me over so
many palpable edges

## OHIO URN

You start out with the neighbors'
air conditioners humming into the fresh Ohio

morning. They are outside you, and this
will do, for subjective purposes. Crane

learned to read here, McGuffey, too.
"Ma-ry had a lit-tle lamb" is how

it runs in the original *Reader*.
Which is to enter the fallen world?

Or no? Each word reflecting the perfection
of its riverine tapestry, fishing poles

from here to Saturday and the
fish eye stared back at consciously and,

not to put too fine a point
on it, dead. Mossy stones, tour

buses idling in the sun, "Cursed
be he who moves these bones" or

should it be "moves these letters"?
But doesn't any writing issue that contract?

Where does that leave us, the nothing
if not mobile readers and writers

moving in delicious obedience to desire
as if time could roll over, play

dead, sit up and beg in one
seamless sentence? The downmarket televangelist on

17 thunders at this theme: "You may
boast of your macho lifestyle. But

on the other side of your
last breath . . ." The Grecian-Urn-like audience sits, I

change channels, each phrase means to change
the culture, and sure, Herbert, take

another breath, a deep one, for
us all. The past says: It was

late August, morning, one of the years,
it was when I was still

a person. I want to learn
the first words for memory, for going

inside and watching light paint the ceiling
and evaporate. There are no such

words. Your last breath, Mom, was
a quick choke. You built my pronouns,

faces, he's and she's people mirror
and live between, before they disappear inside.

## TO MY MOTHER

The sequences are seemingly
   unbreakable chains of seconds,
      which the surroundings demonstrate
        best when left alone,

and so I breathe
   the smell in the
      dark prop plane, feel
        the motors and hear

nothing else, memorialized sense
   carving this from outside,
      the pen lifting from
        the page, a worm

without an apple, a
   truth without a population
      or history to spell
        the names, and from

here I predict a
   future that will stay
      clear of creditors though
        let's keep the sun

airing the streets and
   tuning the messages. In
      this free future there
        are to be no

enemies. All territory the
   shape of a wave.
      Only death to read
        desire's final. Personifications are

faked deaths, I know;
    people are real, me
        too, and I know
            the real one goes

cold at the end,
    it's written into the
        pen stroke I or
            body or language uses

to divide knowledge. Before
    teaching me social location,
        you died and undid
            the difference between now

and then. I touched
    cold forehead, old skin.
        Another lesson I am
            now absent at, abstracted

into sense and memory,
    floating writing in the
        stolen boat it's too
            late to give back.

# THE WOUNDED BOUNDARY

| | |
|---|---|
| I | suck |
| the | twin |
| breasts | of |
| identity | for |
| as | long |
| as | I |
| have | memory |
| of | myself. |
| | |
| There, | where |
| I | was |
| not, | and |
| now | here, |
| the | future |
| masquerades | as |
| present | desire |
| filled | full. |
| | |
| It | really |
| is | a |
| bit | funny |
| the | way |
| things | are |
| and | then |
| are | not. |
| It | sucks, |
| | |
| but | only |
| to | empty |
| the | forms |
| I | need |
| to | fill |
| to | know |

```
the     pleasure
 I      felt.

The     mirror
 is     black
 at     lights
out.    Thought
can't   back
out.
        *You*
*woke*  *me*
 *for*  *that?*
```

## PRODUCT REPRODUCTION

This poem doesn't
even know what
I am telling
it. You

know nothing, do you hear! Nothing! I am looking at

"The Garden of Earthly Delights,"
berries on heads, assholes for
flower vases, and all the
bodies pale, similar, glazed
to keep the pleasure in.
Where's Waldo? Where's

now? I can't tell, and don't
know where our machined
desire fits   ,   but I
   can't ask      you,
   you don't      have a
    clue, do     you?
    And          you're
   the one       that
    gets          to
   speak         later.

   Turn           your
   trick.         Model
your breath      less pregnancy.

# POETRY AND NEWS

Good, I think. That is, if
I can read your writing. There's

something about curving ink that makes
meaning crawl back to the cradle

where fancy lies in wait, its
codicils quaint squiggles the next morning.

It's like reading the weather in
epitaphs. The sound on the page

always about to, a gleam in
the ear, in the dark with

the light on, breathing . . . but night
has fallen deep inside the national

lie, a kind of pocket of
victimized economic membrane, leaking hometown blood.

The green is featureless, the caddy
mutinous. The gatekeeper reads old scores

by the glow under the door.
This is great, and you are

lovely, that is, if I'm reading
your body the way it wants.

Appetites and sirens contrapuntal on the
street. People outside the shelters read

the sentence that says I live,
you live, everybody else can fight

for what's left. Atrocities float above
the depths of the news cycle.

The stringer at the shore drowns
another typo, feeding the calm of

an order floating above its past
like a menu above a terrace.

Dinner and counting stars. Categories are
courtship, of a sort, Jews left,

Armenians right. The palace is up
to something, but the officals keep

filing out. Technically, the day has
been punished enough. Its history has

been smuggled into the sky badly
smudged. Those who can, go home.

## THE REVOLT OF PROCESS

Good, codicils the mutinous. Appetites the
I quaint light The and depths

think. squiggles on, gatekeeper sirens of
That the breathing . . . reads contrapuntal the

is, next but old on news
if morning. night scores the cycle.

I It's has by street. The
can like fallen the People stringer

read reading deep glow outside at
your the inside under the the

writing. weather the the shelters shore
There's in national door. read drowns

something epitaphs. lie, This the another
about The a is sentence typo,

curving sound kind great, that feeding
ink on of and says the

that the pocket you I calm
makes page of are live, of

meaning always victimized lovely, you an
crawl about economic that live, order

back to, membrane, is, everybody floating
to a leaking if else above

the gleam hometown I'm can its
cradle in blood. reading fight past

where the The your for like
fancy ear, green body what's a

lies in is the left. menu
in the featureless, way Atrocies above

wait, dark the it surface a
its with caddy wants. from terrace

Dinner a is filing enough. sky
and sort, up out. Its badly

counting Jews to Technically, history smudged.
stars. left, something, the has Those

Censorship Armenians but day been who
is right. the has smuggled can,

courtship, The officials been into go
of palace keep punished the home.

# IDEAL POEM

And on the street,
ideal readers are
just now giving
birth to the future

while chained to pre-owned
words, structured sentences,
oversexed genres. The semi-

driving by & shooting
are constructive devices
pledging allegiance to
these markers of convenience

continuous buying, yelling,

and indifference, erect
moisture, power made
visible, tucked in, polished,

but swallowed all the same.
One falls into memory
any second, pronoun utopia
frozen into not-quite-foreign

swallowed, ignored,

wars. The ozone-poor, syringe-
tormented, fleshtoned world's
body produces unburied life
and composts it in New Jersey

near Madagascar, while I
myself and you yourself,
we waterslide in post-conscious
media, a choice of channels

and erogenous zones, the
suits of economic armor
walking through the shows
and we can vote for them

as our shame slides
to fear and meets
victorious dreams
turned inside out

on the freeways. It's
not nation time, it's
time to learn languages,
at least one, to start, empezar.

naturalmente los arboles
nos riden y se disaparecen
y nonnaturalmente debemos
estudier ses hojas blancas

## THE WOMB OF AVANT-GARDE REASON

```
            A   P O E M   I S
              I  M  M  O  R
              T A L
       T        n o t  o n l y        B E
    R         because it continues        A
 U           to be read by gene        U
 T           ration after generat    T
 H     ion but because each s Y
      en s i t i v e  r e a d e r,  h a v i n g  e
     x p e r i e n c e d  t h e  p o e m,  a b s o
     r b s  t h e  e x p e r i e n c e  a n d  c o n
     t i n u e s  t o  f e e l  i t.  B U T  N O T
     E V E R Y O N E    F I N D S    I T
      E A S Y  t o  b u y  a l l  t h e  b o o
        k s  h e  w a n t s  a n d  c e r t a i n
        l y  n o  o n e  c a n  c a r r y  h i s
         e n t i r e  l i b r a r y  i n  h i s
          p o c k e t.  I t  i s  f o r
            t h e s e   r e a s o n s
            t h a t  I   h a v e
             c o m p i l e d
             t h e  P o c k
             e t  E d i t
             i o n  o f
             I m m o
             r t a l
            P o e m s
            o f  t h e
            E n g l i s h
            L a n g u a g e.
```

—Oscar Williams

                          The
            last                       thing
        to                                go
            through a fly's
            mind when it hits
            the windshield?
            His asshole.


                    The womb
                      is as
                pretty a process as
                  time has legs
              and hands and learns
          to use them to set poetics
        in the grammar of annoyances,
un-untangleable liens of meant what I didn't want to say
              and where from here?
                  By then it's
                    others.


                      One
                  thousand
                  students
                  and forty
              desks. Who heard?


                    I avant
              You (singular) guard
          He, she, it reads speculatively
(Quick! for the factories and portfolios are full of children)
                    We avant
              You (plural) guard
        They throw tomatoes, bricks, keys, panties

All that
summer,
Father's car was in the garage
with a full tank and the keys
above the visor.


The wind has no clock,
but many frequencies,
each a local call, in material combat with the shrines,
which fight back allegorically, absentmindedly,
and the winds blow the leaves of prophecy
in benediction, contradiction, lifting and sealing
the curtains of memory
rustling their signs and signatories
to reveal the body of the future
wearing only light
and uncoded
immediacy


The words will no longer be utopic settees
in niched rooms,
no more giving comfort
to the enemy within
who sees legibility as a monument lit at night
no more bowing beneath the flourishing arm
of the scene painter perspectively responsible
no more living inside those burning Oedipal circles
with their loops of ashy flame hypnotically extinguished
and reignited, annealing positions
in the aerobic bureaucracy
of personal growth,
no more!

These same flames
have been burning for 200 years
in the dark paternal mills
backlit by the lemony dawn of romantic factories
that increased concentration of surplus emotion in individual psyches
and set personal cupids above every mirror,
replacing an economy of need (masculinized subsistence)
by an economy of desire (feminized superfluity).
Once we have met our needs,
we are free to develop desires,
and desire is infinite.


It branches in phrases,
with no light save what is
with the breezes
blown through capital
to green subjective spaces
trickling down into the inward sense
and outward tastes,
whence, sitting astride every perceived social fence,
I see or saw,
teetering amid time's
teething rhymes,
a natural history of the sublime,
stretching away through the shining wastes
of disembodied economic crime.


If you notice my toga I'll take it off
so that you will notice nothing but my body
and its chosen prosthesis,
its hand, its ear, its mouth, its solar anus,
its Lawrentian phallic godhead, its Kahlo-esque song of its other,
its computer, its macro, its chosen form,
in a word,
its poetics.

And once it's off I'll leave it on the floor shimmering and quivering
and asking to be sensually mourned
and in the performance of said mourning
I will do an unnamed dance to the supersession
of memory to music I will not have to remember
and which, one light day, you may hear.


And pain once buried the path
to pleasure
will articulate itself
along my naked body
and your desire will pull you
toward me and toward the meaning
of all your prior sentences.
And the future will lie down
with the past.


Under the naked aegis
of this spectacular identification
I will swell and connect in unmeasured strains, leaping
with bound feet, found objects
and verbally mandated politics—that's a joke
and you're a great audience—or the next one
will be; and the one after that even better—
deeply in bed with the loftiest leftiest clouds, je ne sais pas,
mujer de mi hijo, hija de mi hija, leaves, hojas,
the never to be seen future
that I keep telling you
sons and daughters
of memory
to study for.

If you notice my toga
I'll take it off
as my prosthesis strums
some object in measured strains
and I'll leave it on the floor
shimmering and quivering to be sensually mourned
and I will do a dance from memory
to music I also am remembering.
Thus the future will shine out
from my naked body
and your desire will pull you
toward me toward the meaning
of your prior sentences.


Tomorrow we empty out
the Grecian Urn:
cardboard, cigarette ends, other testimony
of summer nights, sonnets, confessions,
great honking depictions of the quotidian apocalypse.
We will use Ivory Liquid on it and a gentle
plastic scrubbie because we are, or are to be,
well-meaning and -meant subjects of history.
Numerous intimacies I will only
allude to here have confirmed
that feeling,
bluffing the days off the table,
doubling any bet
any one sentence can make.


My toga on the floor,
sensually mourned,
I do a dance
from memory.
Thursday we'll do Stein & Joyce. Lautréamont & Proust Tuesday.

If any children will be watching
named for the war I couldn't stop
they can be picked up and pointed
specifically at the spectacle
better than a channel changer or meditation or revolution,
excited, held up higher than heads,
higher than the exalted light of lessons,
specially chosen, but, as always seems to happen,
the rhetoric doesn't match the reproduction of cultural values,
something's not quite right, the room is too big,
the echoes too hard to identify with,
anxiety, prayers or sexy dressing take the place
of being able to say the words
in the correct sequences
with the correct tonal values,
you ask Watt
What is Projective Verse
and he answers
Edgar Allen Poe
and Edgar Guest.


Thus Duchamp,
about to die, well, one of these decades anyway,
objectified his desire
by yanking his career down about his knees.
Standing in front of the mirror
he mocked every retina
and sang these words
to the muse of Art History:

Blurb, orbed
hatchery of
the disorder
that is not yet
art and may never be,
so cunning is the indifference
of our enemies, blurb on!
With our neologisms & ye-olde-isms—pray,
theologians and collegians, pray!—
fluttering about our caprisoned heads,
our gender a thing
of the future and our will
driven to market and driving all value
to the necessity of bartering
with geographically uncertain
populations,
to thy meanings
we go, we will go, we have gone.


In thy
desire lie
our jobs.


And squinting
into the camera oscura,
Duchamp
spread the legs of patriarchal poetry
and begot reason and reason
begot sensibility and sensibility
begot eroticism and eroticism
begot poetics and poetics
begot schools.

It was just before
the war.
My privates had been on display
throughout the prior decade:
marching merchandising and simply putting up
with being screwed by beings
you could see but couldn't be.


They're on tv,
they're on the tips of our tongues
and the salt of wit begins to taste nasty,
a sort of of toxic backdrop of reasons not to take out the garbage
because A, it's not our turn, B, there's no place to put it
and C, it's all garbage out there anyway,
oceans airwaves soundtracks landfill anthologies;
and B, again, I am, and you are, simply grammatically,
RSVP or nay, Armageddon or Sarajevo,
and that's all there's time for,
so plague me no plagues, sky us no skies,
and keep your eyes
on the moving stream of words.


One two three on up to five hundred thousand
I told a story they gave me troops
I hardly had to ask
not many wanted to be among them
but they went out and did
what they thought they couldn't have been told to do.

And I thank and spank them and dance
inwardly between their chosen words:
a still small voice
in the hard-pressed leisure centers
spreading shame and glory throughout the body,
a singing telegram announcing a self-owned slavery
that needs to train permanently and a reason
to tame the voices, and press the word shavings into a mold:
let the head wear its hair thoughtfully
and stylize its openings.


The dance—my only memory—
was named for a round of peace talks
that never got to the ground.
They simply hovered with a helicopter's
edginess in plain sight
until the mountain that was
formed by castoff lifeforms was deserted,
though its outlines suggested paradise.


I described one particular city
so thoroughly I literally wiped it
off the map so I don't remember where it was
or what I wanted because I don't look anything
like I did
or if I do
I don't remember.
Do you?

Reproduction or critique.
Reproduction of critique.
I was really local that night.
I gave Mina's underwear to Frank to smell;
later when he started wearing them
I began to read him seriously.


Perhaps you get the impression that I prophecy at random,
weaving the falls of memory into a kind of
permeable dream slush fund payable to no known account
and sayable in no known accent, perhaps
my genderectomies disrupt your pleasure differentials,
my pessaries and sacramental stogies fallen under the couch
and wrapped in the merest shimmer of cat hair make you fear
that the ultimate destination of identity will be necklaced
with extreme irony, the most rigorously personal
fateful aleatory taste die with your days,
temporally mourned, as impossible to reorganize
as to piece back your liver, your first view
of an expressway, vehicles produced by desires, producing desires,
themselves the leftovers of desires,
when you thought you would be left over, too.


They will die
last night.
We have lived
tomorrow.

*The absence of theory has seized the masses,* Adorno

CHAPTER ONE

OBEDIENT PLIES OF WRITING SO FLEXIBLY THIN THEY'LL SAY ANYTHING EXCEPT AFTERWARDS.

HISTORY GLIMMERS OUT OF A PAST ONE PART REPRIEVE AND TWENTY PARTS EXECUTED DESIRE.

# IT HIDES IN THE SHAPES.

## WHAT'S MISSING CENTERS AROUND YOU,

## LAUNDERED ENCLAVE OF SENSATION,

## LIBIDINOUS CORPORATION OF BODY PARTS,

CRASH-TESTED BY THE LATEST INVOLUNTARY MEMORIES,

## REFLEXES MUDDLING THROUGH,

RETINAS CURVED AROUND THE VANISHING POINT.

A SKY FALLEN ONTO THE MORNING PAPER,

UNFOLDED TO GIVE TERROR A HUMAN FACE

# AND SHOW IT IN A POEM.

# POEM! THE VERY WORD

# IS A SHTETL PHOTOGRAPHED,

ITS ACCENTS REMOVED NOW FROM ALL CHANGE.

## THE WIND STILL BLOWS FROM THE FUTURE

BUT THE ERA OF THE SINGLEHANDED SENTENCE IS NEARING ITS CLOSE.

HOW MANY DIVISIONS ARE YOU STANDING IN FRONT OF?

CHAPTER TWO

Where language is, there
    I was once, infant,
        everywhere, held in the
            devices of an enchanter

who smiled, hand over
    heart, pledging perception's daintiest
        favors, far back and
            fast forward. The jailers

are in eternity, too,
    with their pieces of
        cake that have nourished
            our formulas for pleasure

for so long now,
    the past humps up
        until it can only be
            guessed at, tangled in

the bedclothes. Dark morning,
    the whippers burning in
        the sconces, eager for
            a full day's work.

## CHAPTER THREE

no ovens
no ships
no showers
no whips

no scalpels
no pliers
no genealogies
no wires

no salt water
no rope
no chairs
no files

no chambers
no gutters
no trenches
no ditches

But we live in a land where the laugh track floods,
the candidates rise above class,
ties loose, chests there to be beaten,
where the wind blows free for the first month,
after that some charges apply.

## CHAPTER FOUR

The absence of theory pulses in my neck,
at least I've thought so,
sitting on the edge of the bed, pulling off my socks.
Break the life-mask of empiricism and, underneath, prophecies
become visible: the death of the past, swaddled in
old jargons of self-expression, those other bodies.

The next layer down we find a typewriter,
at least in my case,
the platen nubbled in a grid where the breath habitually roosted.
So you work away, dusting and smashing alteratively,
a kind of rhythmic settling of ever older scores
like an eye sinking into its socket.

## CHAPTER FIVE

Which reminds me. There was this
South Seas island, and in the

alley, after the shows, they'd gather,
to wait for the stars. So

this one person is there, staring
at the bricks, not really seeing

them, the invisibility of the obvious,
et cetera, etc. In some versions,

they're classes. Class: I met some
of my best friends in class.

And so the one brick says
to the other brick, "You ever

see a shrink? And the second
brick says, If I saw a

shrink the whole wall would be
in big trouble. And the first

brick says, I hate to be
the one to break the news,

but you're not that important. And
brick number two says, Touché, and

big deal, too. Touché away all
day, and I'd hardly feel it.

But how about you? Did you
ever see a shrink? And the

first brick says, Yes, it so
happens that I did, one time.

I go in there and the
shrink says, You need to find

the inner you, that'll be one
hundred dollars, and I say, You're

kidding, the inner me is in
no way different from the outer

me, if you don't know that
from the get-go then what am

I doing here? Touché, says the
shrink, you're right, it's been a

long day, and you're not my
last brick. And then I say,

Now if you're going to be
asking for my sympathy then you

should be paying me, how about
we make it ninety bucks, because

I'm not one to copy your
material. Ha ha, says the shrink,

but that one I've heard before.
No, what I meant to say

is you've got to find the
real you. Forget inner. Real hooks

up with the material conditions among
which consciousness undergoes its traumas and

desires, and it can lose its
shape, easily. Well, I say, I've

heard that one before, and it
was in a better version, too.

I mean, "material conditions among which
consciousness"—who do you think is

still listening at that point? You're supposed
to be helping people, not getting

it, whatever "it" is, right, whatever
"right" is, so the teacher won't

take out his red pen and
get your paper all bloody.

CHAPTER SIX

Anyway, the way the better version
goes is when you say, That'll

be one hundred dollars, then I
say, When I find the real

me I'll get him to pay
you, and then you're supposed to

say, It's not that simple,—Wait,
how does it go from here?

Ah but that's why you're here,
interrupts the shrink, to get access

to those repressed memories. Then maybe
you can find the real you.

Shut up, I explain, so I
can remember how it goes. You

say, It's not that simple . . . Wait.
Oh yes. Then I say in

answer to that, You're right, who
knows who is who, I don't

know who I am, and you
don't know who I am, I

could be anybody, I could be
you, maybe I owe myself one

hundred dollars, who knows? and maybe
you're me and you owe me

one hundred dollars, who can say,
but I'll tell you what we

can do, let's just split the
difference, you give me fifty and

we can call the whole thing off.


CHAPTER SEVEN

Which except for the usual allowances
is pretty much exactly the way

I heard it," says the brick.
And speaking of identity. Once there

was a Jew, a Serb and
a Samoan, in a lightbulb, when

it starts raining, first only a
few drops. But it turns out

that one stands for ten, ten
means a hundred, and then the

uncountable masses of others who maybe
kick your skull around if you

get too close. In some versions
it's a soccer ball. A whistle

blows. You touch my mirror and
boom: Seven centuries of annoyed family

epics, nothing but episodic payback with
crescendoing spirals of blood blocking exactly

the same arteries and messing exactly
the same stony thoroughfares. This thinking

with things as they exist, what
good does it do anyone not

yet born? Back in my century,
back in the matter with me,

I flew, like other poets, we
signed our letters and sold them,

kept them, lost them, gave our
love to particular people, meant by

this something like I'm touching the
keys and this once they are

not as cold as some medieval
suet, blessed and eaten, damned and

waiting for the future where the
dead are already buried en masse

by judgments already made, beneath lobs
of fundamental meaning smashing bridges with

aimless accuracy, probing the most removed
non-readers for the smell of their

heirs. Give my love to their
particular cases in particular places, which

I can't see from here and
so I also have to lob

the whole mass forward with undifferentiated
obsessesiveness, into what looks illegible. Until one

day, a day that will
never die, since it only exists

in the past and the future,
with my body blocking the otherwise

perfect symmetry,

# THE MASQUE OF RHYME

Adding my pee to the sea
of rhyme, it's time I admit sameness

is a bit of a hoax.
Yes, my body lies over social oceans

like yours and slightly like Rover's,
except he barks to speak and we

speak to bargain and intermingle. All's
translation in love and war. Do you

hear the joke about the marriage of
true mind to impediment after impediment?

That's what we call "language," at
least around here. What rhymes with "rhythm"?

"Mythic"? You have to squint to
hear it. Squint and scatter letters to

the five senses, shake off circumstance, and
find yourself in words: squatting amid

ashes while the wicked affluent legislators
dress for the ball. Your feet ache

and stink. The thought-track wakes and thinks:
novelty again, the same old novelty.

It's almost worse than royalty. My biographic
foot in the glass shoe—fate

or déjà vu? The rhythm of
days produces chill, stupor, and after considerable

training, a bunch of personal pronouns.
It's Thursday, history's late as usual. Meanwhile,

some sort of sexual traffic jam
has been goading us all into public

revelation. Offstage, Fact slapped Value on the
butt, and said, Break a leg,

make a killing, show those suckers
where to suck. And Value answered, Don't

be vulgar, Fact, unless you're speaking personally.
As for me, where the bee

sucks, there suck I, a mean-er,
a be-er, an arriviste tooling down that

divided highway heading where none, they say,
ever returns. And when I don't

come back, say I told you
everything about yourself except the future, lie

alone in our bed of roses
whence, they say, poems arise, to amuse

the students when we've gone to prose.
I'd say more but you hear

those stuck horns blaring: that's been
my cue ever since I can remember.

# ROOF BOOKS (Partial List)

Andrews, Bruce. **EX WHY ZEE**. 112p. $10.95.

Andrews, Bruce. **Getting Ready To Have Been Frightened**. 116p. $7.50.

Benson, Steve. **Blue Book**. Copub. with The Figures. 250p. $12.50

Bernstein, Charles. **Islets/Irritations**. 112p. $9.95.

Bernstein, Charles (editor). **The Politics of Poetic Form**. 246p. $12.95; cloth $21.95.

Brossard, Nicole. **Picture Theory**. 188p. $11.95.

Child, Abigail. **Scatter Matrix**. 79p. $9.95.

Davies, Alan. **Active 24 Hours**. 100p. $5.

Davies, Alan. **Signage**. 184p. $11.

Davies, Alan. **Rave**. 64p. $7.95.

Day, Jean. **A Young Recruit**. 58p. $6.

Di Palma, Ray. **Motion of the Cypher**. 112p. $10.95.

Di Palma, Ray. **Raik**. 100p. $9.95.

Doris, Stacy. **Kildare**. 104p. $9.95.

Dreyer, Lynne. **The White Museum**. 80p. $6.

Edwards, Ken. **Good Science**. 80p. $9.95.

Eigner, Larry. **Areas Lights Heights**. 182p. $12, $22 (cloth).

Gizzi, Michael. **Continental Harmonies**. 92p. $8.95.

Gottlieb, Michael. **Ninety-Six Tears**. 88p. $5.

Grenier, Robert. **A Day at the Beach**. 80p. $6.

Grosman, Ernesto. **The XUL Reader:**
   **An Anthology of Argentine Poetry (1981–1996)**. 167p. $14.95.

Hills, Henry. **Making Money**. 72p. $7.50. VHS videotape $24.95. Book & tape $29.95.

Huang Yunte. **SHI: A Radical Reading of Chinese Poetry.** 76p. $9.95

Hunt, Erica. **Local History**. 80 p. $9.95.

Inman, P. **Criss Cross**. 64 p. $7.95.

Inman, P. **Red Shift**. 64p. $6.

Lazer, Hank. **Doublespace**. 192 p. $12.

Mac Low, Jackson. **Representative Works: 1938–1985**. 360p. $12.95, $18.95 (cloth).

Mac Low, Jackson. **Twenties**. 112p. $8.95.

Moriarty, Laura. **Rondeaux**. 107p. $8.

Neilson, Melanie. **Civil Noir**. 96p. $8.95.

Pearson, Ted. **Planetary Gear**. 72p. $8.95.

Perelman, Bob. **Virtual Reality**. 80p. $9.95.

Piombino, Nick, **The Boundary of Blur**. 128p. $13.95.

Raworth, Tom. **Clean & Will-Lit**. 106p. $10.95.

Robinson, Kit. **Balance Sheet**. 112p. $9.95.

Robinson, Kit. **Ice Cubes**. 96p. $6.

Scalapino, Leslie. **Objects in the Terrifying Tense Longing from Taking Place.**
   88p. $9.95.

Seaton, Peter. **The Son Master**. 64p. $5.

# ROOF BOOKS (Partial List Continued)

Sherry, James. **Popular Fiction**. 84p. $6.
Silliman, Ron. **The New Sentence**. 200p. $10.
Silliman, Ron. **N/O**. 112p. $10.95.
Stephans, Brian Kim. **Free Space Comix**.
Templeton, Fiona. **Cells of Release**. 128p. with photographs. $13.95.
Templeton, Fiona. **YOU—The City**. 150p. $11.95.
Ward, Diane. **Human Ceiling**. 80p. $8.95.
Ward, Diane. **Relation**. 64p. $7.50.
Watten, Barrett. **Progress**. 122p. $7.50.
Weiner, Hannah. **We Speak Silent**. 76 p. $9.95
Yasusada, Araki. **Doubled Flowering: From the Notebooks of Araki Yasusada**. 272p. $14.95.